W9-CZM-274

PRAISES FOR
REUNITING WITH MOTHER

"Interesting and relatable story. The encounter with Geneva was compelling, and I enjoyed the writing more and more as it went on." **~Phoebe Shanahan, MA in English Literature**

"There is a saying claiming that those who insist persevere and that is exactly the motto of *Reuniting with Mother*." **~Dimitra Manda, BA in English Language and Literature, English Teacher**

"I love this story! It is touching and very well-written. The author's reunion with her mother was very emotional, while evoking some feelings of joy. This story will touch the hearts of many. A must read!" **~Jean Smith, Spring, TX**

"The author understands that her mother has a mental illness, so she is patient, not pushy." **~Kristen Driskill, Belton, MO**

"I like the author's journey and how she was patient with her mother." **~Ana Wells, Raymore, MO**

During the time period of this story, the author was very aware that her mother had a mental illness. However, she did not know her actual diagnosis.

Dr. Grace LaJoy Henderson

FINDING MOTHER SERIES

REUNITING

WITH

MOTHER

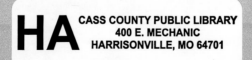
A Story of Tenacity

Inspirations by Grace LaJoy
Raymore, MO 64083

REUNITING WITH MOTHER: A STORY OF TENACITY
Grace LaJoy Henderson

Disclaimer. I have tried to recreate events, locales and conversations from my memories of them. In order to maintain their anonymity in some instances I have changed the names of individuals and places. I may have changed some identifying characteristics and details such as physical properties, occupations and places of residence.

Due to the delicate subject of mental illness, all names are fictitious. I have taken great precaution to ensure my mother could not be located, while still sharing my real-life story.

Mission. Sharing my story to help increase awareness of mental illness.

Goal. Reducing stigma. Fostering connection. Inspiring hope.

REUNITING WITH MOTHER: A STORY OF TENACITY
Copyright 2020. Grace LaJoy Henderson
Written by Grace LaJoy Henderson
Published by Inspirations by Grace LaJoy
Raymore, MO 64083

ISBN: 978-1-7341868-4-0

Printed in the United States of America

DEDICATION

To my three brothers, "Jerome," "Grayson," and "Terrance." It was awesome to be able to travel with you all to reunite with our mother. I feel grateful that we were together during that emotional experience.

To my two sisters, "Carla" and "Danisha." I wish the two of you could have been present at the reunion.

To my two children, Aric and Arica. Thank you so much for your support throughout the years and especially during my reunion with Geneva

To my mother, "Geneva," who I finally saw again after forty-nine years.

ACKNOWLEDGEMENT

The *Finding Mother Series* is my own recollection of my siblings' and my reunion with our mother after forty-nine years. When referring to my father, mother and siblings, I use fictitious names, as this is *my* story to tell. Their accounts may be different, as they may have perceived things from a different angle.

ABOUT THE SERIES

The *Finding Mother Series* is a complex, touching opportunity for readers to see into the author's journey to find her mother after decades. This series would be ideal for students at a secondary level who are searching for insight about the emotional conflicts and battles one must face when someone they care about has a mental illness. The four books in the series are segmented to provide specific lenses to the overall process, with a number of opportunities available for opening discussions about mental illness from both the author's point of view and her mother's.
~Leslie Arambula, MA Creative Writing, English Teacher

A WORD FROM THE AUTHOR
ABOUT THE FINDING MOTHER SERIES

Stories like mine are common and there is a sincere need to establish dialogue concerning this issue.

When I asked my mother how she felt about me publishing our reunion story, she laughed and said, "I guess it will be alright." Then she laughed again. She seemed flattered. Therefore, I really want her to feel proud about the way I present my recollection of the story. I told her I would not be revealing her real name or location.

To protect my mother's privacy, I have not revealed the full name under which she was found. I would never have found her under the name listed in my original foster care storybook. I believe that my personal recollection of our reunion details will inspire you. I hope it will decrease the stigma of mental illness in order to promote helpful discussion about this subject.

Due to my own personal struggle with the stigma surrounding mental illness, initially, I was only going to share the positive details of finding and reuniting with my mother. I did not intend to share any of the parts that were embarrassing for me. However, when others heard my story of how I found my mother after five decades, they told me they felt inspired. Many had similar stories. Realizing my personal story was intriguing, and could be helpful to so many people, I am sharing it...all of it.

REUNITING WITH MOTHER: A STORY OF TENACITY
Grace LaJoy Henderson

TABLE OF CONTENTS

REUNITING WITH MOTHER: A STORY OF TENACITY
Grace LaJoy Henderson

FOREWORD

Secondary students would absolutely benefit from this book.

One skill that I would like to see increased in our students, is conflict resolution. As educators, we must do our part to ensure that we are equipping our students with the proper skills to become competent and productive members of society. Conflict is a guarantee as our youth transition from students to adulthood, so it is vital for them to learn how to handle the situations that cause it and advocate for themselves, while remaining respectful and understanding. This book provides a great example of that.

~**Jacob Kelow, M.S.Ed.**
Secondary School Counselor
Kansas City Public Schools

PREFACE

After I had located my mother, my three brothers and I traveled to meet her for the first time in forty-nine years. While we were out of town, we made three visits to the boarding home where she lives. In *Reuniting with Mother*, I uncover what happened during each of the visits and reveal my account of the events.

To help you follow the story a little better, my father and mother had six children together. Here are the fictitious names for each of them as shared in the story: Jerome, Grayson, Carla, Terrance, Danisha and myself, Grace. The story will reveal why my two sisters were not with us during the reunion.

INTRODUCTION

After I found my mother, there was only one thing I desired: to reunite with her as soon as I could! Thoughts of seeing her after all of these years were overwhelming. To look her in the face and tell her how much I had longed to meet her again was my heart's sincere desire.

I was experiencing bouts of disbelief. Is this moment for real? Was that actually my own mother that I spoke with on the phone? I found solace in knowing my brother, Jerome had spoken to her, too, and he believed it to be her.

REUNITING WITH MOTHER: A STORY OF TENACITY
Grace LaJoy Henderson

Chapter 1

AFTER FINDING MOTHER

As soon as Jerome and I felt comfortable that we had indeed found our missing mother, we decided to share our news with our other siblings. Jerome informed Grayson of the news while I told Terrance.

That night when I told my two children that I had finally found my mother, their grandmother, I could barely keep my emotions at bay.

My daughter could not believe I had found her after all of those years. She was extremely happy for me, but she had gotten used to not having a maternal grandmother so she did not feel the need to go and unite with her immediately.

My son was shocked, too. "That is amazing!" he said. He was very joyful for me but, like my daughter, he did not feel a connection with his newly found grandmother. So, he did not have a deep interest in rushing to meet her either.

I understood where they both stood. However, it was eye-opening to witness my children not sharing the same endearment towards my mother as I felt.

I was ready to go to her right away.

I had waited forty-nine years and did not want to wait one minute longer.

I considered renting a car and driving out of town immediately that very night or early the next morning. Basically, as fast as humanly possible.

When I informed my daughter, son and brother, Terrance, of my intent to travel right away, they each warned me of a winter storm warning in the area where my mother lives, and encouraged me not to drive.

I felt frustrated. I had finally found my mother, now here was yet another obstacle to overcome.

They suggested I should take a plane instead since it would get me there quicker anyway. Driving would be a seventeen plus hour drive, while the plane would be only a three-hour trip. I took heed of their warnings and decided to wait until after the foul weather had passed. During my wait, I made up my mind that I was going to travel there by plane.

There was only one problem: purchasing a plane ticket at such short notice would be expensive.

Excited about me finally finding my mother, my daughter paid all my expenses to reunite with her, which included my plane ticket. "Let me know if you need anything else" she told me.

Grace LaJoy Henderson

Due to the winter storm warning, I was left in limbo wondering what day would be the best day to travel. Realizing I could not leave immediately and that I would be traveling by plane, my brothers and I discussed the possibility of traveling together.

The big question for me was, "When can we leave?"

I only got a couple hours of sleep that night, worrying about how soon I would be able to get out of town to see my mother.

The next morning, I received a group text from Jerome suggesting we leave that upcoming Thursday, March 8th and return on Sunday, March 11th. His text put me at ease. It put us all on the same page. I was able to calm down knowing we would all be together during this very emotional experience.

I texted him back informing him that, "this sounds good to me." We discussed our plans by text and phone until we finally agreed on the details of our flight, hotel, and rental car.

From the afternoon of March 3rd until the morning of March 8th, I eagerly awaited the moment that my brothers and I would finally board the plane.

Ironically, on March 5th, I received an email from the private investigator that I had contacted just days before I had found my mother. I had told him of my failed attempts to find my mother and asked if maybe he could help me find my siblings.

REUNITING WITH MOTHER: A STORY OF TENACITY
Grace LaJoy Henderson

Well, in his email, he asked me if I would still like for him to look into finding my siblings, and possibly even my mother. He said he was willing to "put some time into the matter, but can't guarantee anything." He said he believed he had some solid leads and all I had to do was to give him a few hundred dollars to get started.

Feeling as if he was trying to take advantage of me, I was happy to respond to his email, letting him know I had already found my mother and that I was preparing to go out of town to reunite with her.

The night before the trip, I packed everything I needed. I also packed some pictures. I found it difficult to choose among my photos and I wondered how many would be enough. At first, I thought I would only take some pictures of my two children and myself. Then I decided to throw in a few more of my father, brothers and sisters and their children. I did not think I would need all of those. I just felt it would be better to have too many than not enough.

After I was all packed, I took a shower and put on the outfit I was going to wear. I woke up at two o'clock the next morning and put my suitcase in my car. By three o'clock, I was driving to my brother Terrance's house to ride with him to the airport. When I arrived at his house, he took my suitcase out of my car and put it in his truck. We drove to pick up our other brother, Grayson so we could all ride to the airport together. We pulled up at Grayson's home and Terrance got out of the truck and helped him put his suitcases in the back.

Finally, we were on our way to the airport.

My third brother, Jerome, was traveling from another state. He was going to meet us there. After takeoff, our plane flew from Kansas City to a connecting flight.

While we were in the air, I remembered how my father would say, "If you all ever want to look for her, I will take you. But, she may not receive you all."

Therefore, I had no idea what to expect or if she would even talk to us. However, there was one thing I knew: that I was extremely excited.

I felt that however things went down, I would be satisfied just for having found her.

We were sitting on the plane after landing at the connecting airport. I was in between Terrance and Grayson. We were feeling restless, eager, and somewhat fearful of what was to come when we finally reached our destination.

As we waited for permission to get off the plane, I pulled out my phone and began recording a video of myself talking about how I was feeling at that moment.

I stated, "I am very tired and anxious, yet nervous."

REUNITING WITH MOTHER: A STORY OF TENACITY
Grace LaJoy Henderson

I was feeling zealous as I awaited the moment that our travel would finally come to an end, resulting with us being in the presence of our dear mother.

"Are you all okay with being on camera?" I asked my brothers.

"Yes, that is fine," Terrance replied.

Grayson felt a little shy as he laughed, "Oh, go ahead, I don't mind."

"So, how are you guys feeling right now?" I asked.

Terrance was sitting on my left, so I aimed my camera phone towards his face first.

Looking into the camera, he said, "I'm ready to be finished flying."

Then I turned to my right.

Grayson stated, "I'm tired and sleepy, but I am ready to see my mom!"

I felt anxious to get off the plane and board the next plane.

When we got off the plane for our layover, we were all hungry, so we bought some food, sat in the airport food court and ate before we finally boarded the connected flight, which would land us in the same location as our mother!

We sat patiently on the plane as it rolled up the runway, into the air, and above the clouds. To keep from feeling bored or anxious, I slept and worked some puzzles until finally our plane was preparing to land. My enthusiasm was immeasurable and I could not wait. Gazing out of the window, I saw one of the large wings of the plane and the clouds below us. I watched as the plane began to maneuver down into the clouds, then out, and slowly down onto the runway.

I could hardly believe that we had actually arrived!

As I looked out of the airplane window, I could see remaining snow on the ground from the snowstorm I had heard about before we left Kansas City.

The plane stopped and finally we were able to get off the plane.

As we walked through the airport to go pick up our rental car, I said a short prayer hoping that everything would go well and that our mother would receive us. I uttered that prayer because I was afraid that my father's warning all those years back might come to be true. Had I really come that far only to have my mother refuse to see any of us? I dreaded the thought that my greatest fear may become a reality. After we had rented the car, we drove to our hotel where we met up with Jerome, who had purchased a separate rental car. As soon as we finished checking into our rooms and freshening up, we all got in one vehicle and drove to the address where our mother was.

REUNITING WITH MOTHER: A STORY OF TENACITY
Grace LaJoy Henderson

We did not know what to expect. However, we were all very eager to be on our way to see our mother after forty-nine years!

Our drive to the place where our mother lived was long and traffic was heavy. Other drivers on the road did not provide right-of-way due to everyone trying to make ways for themselves in the hectic traffic. A drive that was supposed to be only twenty-minutes turned into an hour long. I thought we would *never* arrive.

We finally pulled up to the boarding home around four thirty in the afternoon. We parked our car in this very old, unkempt neighborhood.

Before going in, we sat in the car and contemplated about whether or not she would receive us. We thought maybe she would since Jerome and I had spoken with her on the phone. "Come see me," she had told us.

We finally got out of the car and began walking toward the large, old looking two-story boarding home. We paced carefully in the snow towards the front door.

Residents of the home were sitting and standing outside on the front porch and steps smoking cigarettes. Their coats and clothes were old and tattered. They all turned around and stared at us as we continued towards the house. While we were persisting in the direction of the smokers, I scanned their faces with hopes one of them was my mother. None of them appeared to be her.

As we walked in between them to get to the front door, one of the men asked if we had some spare change we could give him.

One of my brothers happily reached into his pocket and gave the man some change.

We entered the house, walked through a strong foul odor, over to the front office and asked for April. A woman named Ashley told us that April had gotten off work at four o'clock, so we had just missed her. April originally wanted to be there to make sure our mother, Geneva, would be comfortable with our visit. Since she was not there, Ashley took us back to Geneva's bedroom.

The hallway back to her room was dim, and not well lit.

The less than one-minute walk to her room felt more like five minutes.

Finally, I was getting ready to see the face of the woman who carried me in her stomach for nine months, for whom I had spent most of my life searching. I could not wait to see what she looked like.

REUNITING WITH MOTHER: A STORY OF TENACITY
Grace LaJoy Henderson

Chapter 2

SEEING MOTHER AFTER 49 YEARS

We entered the room where Geneva sat on her bed wearing black jeans, a black skullcap and a grey fleece jacket under a black leather coat as if she was getting ready to go outdoors.

There were three beds in that room. I remembered April had told me she shared the bedroom with two other women, one of which was in the room. She was a heavy-set younger woman.

The tiny, older woman sitting on the bed, who was my mother, did not look the way I had always imagined she would.

I had a picture of her in my mind based off a young adult picture, in her late twenties, which I had kept since I was a little girl. The picture I had portrayed a woman who was well dressed, with styled hair, a round face with a smooth complexion, light colored skin, slightly slanted eyes, full lips, white teeth and a bright, beautiful smile.

The woman who I was looking at looked like the exact opposite and had the appearance of someone who lacked the necessities of life.

The cap she was wearing covered the frizzy grey hair that was sticking out on each side. Her face was oval-shaped, with a weary look in her eyes and only a few teeth left.

Seeing what she looked like brought back memories of how, as a young child, I desired to take care of her. I wanted to find her, bring her home and give her all of the love she deserved. As I stared at this estranged woman, I thought, "If she had been in my life, she would not look this way."

I had always thought I would recognize my mother if I ever saw her. I thought she would look just like me and that I would know immediately that she was my mother. Honestly, I do not know why, but I thought she would be taller.

This little woman was contrary to what I had expected.

All of a sudden, I felt unsure if she was actually our mother. In that moment, I began to feel fearful that we might have traveled all of those miles just to reunite with a woman who was not our mother!

As soon as my siblings and I saw her sitting there, we immediately began to try to determine if this was our mother by asking her questions like, "What is your middle name?" and "What was your mother's first name?" and "Do you remember living in Kansas City, Missouri?"

She seemed afraid and overwhelmed by all of our questions. She looked up at my three big and tall brothers, then

24

glared at me and said, "I don't know who you are. I'm not going to talk to anybody because I don't know you all."

We explained our belief that we were her children who she left in Kansas City almost fifty years ago. We told her we did not want anything from her, that we missed her and wanted to see her.

She looked at each of us again, and just when it appeared she might actually accept us as her children, she said, "You are not my people. Anybody can come in here and say they are my people."

Just then, her roommate exclaimed, "Geneva, these *are* your people! They look *just like* you and they have pictures of you."

"What do you have to do with that?" Geneva asked her roommate.

Then she turned back to us and said, "You all are strangers. I don't talk to strangers about anything personal. I'm not giving out any information unless I know who I am talking to."

We asked her what it would take for her to know.

She just looked at us and did not answer.

I told her I brought my birth certificate.

She looked at me as if she might be interested in seeing my birth certificate. Then she said, "No, I don't want to see that."

Just then, I reached into a bag that I had carried in, pulled out a gift, and showed it to her. "Ms. Geneva, I brought you a brand new, soft throw blanket. I will just leave it here," I said, as I went to place it on the bed next to hers.

Despite looking tempted to accept it, she said, "No, I don't want that." Feeling saddened and let down, I put the gift back into my bag.

In our disappointment, my brother Jerome and I asked her, "Do you remember speaking with us over the phone? You told us to come see you." We assured her she did not owe us anything, that we were not looking for any apologies, that we loved her and just wanted to see her.

She said, "No, I don't trust that," and continued to stare back and forth at each one of us, as if she wanted to get a really good look at what we all looked like. After skimming each of our faces, she did not receive us, just as my father had cautioned so many years ago.

I must admit, although I believed my father back then, there was a part of me that felt he may have been saying that out of his anger towards her. However, in that moment, I was actually witnessing the truth for myself; and it was sadly disappointing.

I felt like this would probably be the last time I would ever see her, so I took a really good look at her.

Our pleading with her to accept us seemed useless.

Finally, in a moment of sadness, Terrance announced, "I'm done. It has been so long, who cares anyway?"

With that said, we all turned towards the door of the bedroom and walked out with our heads held down feeling rejected and heartbroken. All the money we had spent, the time on the plane, the excitement, hope and anticipation we had while traveling turned into great despair and disappointment within a matter of minutes.

I could not believe this was happening. I felt devastated as we made our way towards the front door.

Ashley followed us outside. She was very nice and kind to us. We all stood on the sidewalk in front of the boarding home. She listened to how we felt about our mother not accepting us and she tried to encourage us.

She reminded us that our mother had a mental illness and that she may just need time to accept us since it had been so long since she had seen us.

Ashley claimed that Geneva never talks to her and that she usually has a hard time getting her to take her medication, whereas April had given us a completely different account.

Like April, Ashley was helpful and caring towards us. She acted very concerned about us having a successful reunion with our mother.

I told Ashley that I really wish April had been there. I felt strongly that we would have had a better outcome if she had been.

Ashley apologized to us for April's absence.

Anyhow, I wanted to come back the next day because I at least wanted to see what would happen if April was there.

She told us April would be there at eight o'clock the next morning and we were welcome to come back.

After finally walking away from the boarding home, we sat in the rental car with an "I give up" and "forget this!" attitude. Then, we all spent a few minutes talking about what we had just experienced.

I noticed my brother Terrance looked more like our mother than I had ever realized. Growing up, people always said my brother Grayson and I looked more like our mother than the rest of my siblings. However, I did not see Grayson nor myself in my mother's face at all. It was amazing to see what my mother looked like and which of my siblings looked like her.

After the comparisons, the sad fact remained we had just been rejected by our mother once again.

After some consideration, I said, "We should come back tomorrow, when April is here. Perhaps April can be of help to us."

After talking about it for a few minutes, we all agreed to return the next day and try once again to woo our mother into accepting us. We concluded that we had not traveled all of those miles just to give up now.

We drove back to our hotel and did our best to relax our minds. Grayson and Terrance went out to eat dinner together, while Jerome and I opted for a quiet dinner at the hotel.

At some point after we made our decision to return the following day, a very strong feeling of rejection came over me and I just wanted to leave and go back home to Kansas City as soon as I could. A distraught feeling caused me to actually forgot we had agreed to go back to try again the next day. My high hopes had somehow vanished and I shared my feelings with Jerome during dinner.

I cannot figure out why I suddenly gave up after being so adamant about us going back the next day. I just know that during our drive from the boarding home to the hotel, I replayed this one thing in my mind: The way Geneva looked each of us in the face and rejected us without any remorse. I absolutely did not like the woman who we had just encountered, and I did not want her as my mother.

After dinner, I retreated to my hotel room then called to tell my daughter and cousin how the reunion visit had gone.

Afterwards, I recorded a video of myself talking about how I felt. I had been recording my excitement about the trip ever since we were leaving Kansas City. I initially hoped to create an inspirational documentary of what I hoped would be a wonderful heartfelt meeting with our mother.

REUNITING WITH MOTHER: A STORY OF TENACITY
Grace LaJoy Henderson

When things turned out to be disappointing, I thought, "I'm not recording my feelings about this." However, I felt like, "It is what it is." Therefore, even though things had not gone as calculated, I hesitantly recorded my negative reaction to a reunion-gone-wrong.

I talked about the heartbreaking situation we had just experienced; and how April had stated if Geneva were *her* mother, they would live together in the same home.

The woman I saw did not look like the woman April had described.

I expressed how we were standing there, in front of our mother, listening to her as she told us we were not her people; how devastating that was for me; and how I felt worse for my brothers because I could see they were hurting and I could do nothing to help them.

While venting, I wondered what was worse, not knowing where my mother was, or knowing where she is and knowing that she did not accept me.

After recording my misery, I lay there feeling heartbroken, trying to see a positive side to having found her. I no longer had to search for her, speculate about where she could be, or wonder why I do not have a mother.

Witnessing her living in a state of poverty and suffering from a mental illness helped me to understand why she left us.

Nevertheless, it still hurt deeply.

I had always blamed my father for her leaving, but after this failed reunion, I was placing all the blame on her. This experience had left me feeling rejected because I had finally come face-to-face with my mother only to have her deny me.

In my pain, I thought back about our final few moments at the boarding home. Although I did not think I looked anything like Geneva, I noticed one similarity. She kept biting her lips. *I* bite *my* lips! I have always known I copied the habit from someone but could not, for the life of me remember from whom I had copied it. Observing Geneva, it was clear I had copied it from her before she left us back when I was two.

That night, I spent hours on the phone with the airline and rental car company trying to find a way to leave and head back to Kansas City. A smooth exit was not possible, so I finally put my head on my pillow to rest for three hours before it was time to wake up again the next morning.

When morning came, my brothers and I had breakfast together in the hotel dining room.

While eating, Grayson asked me about my desire to return home. "I thought we had all agreed to go back to see Mother today."

That moment felt like a wakeup call urging me to remember our agreement. I told him I was in so much emotional pain after our first visit that I had actually forgotten our decision. "We should definitely go back and try again," I told him.

After breakfast, Jerome spoke with his mother-in-law on the phone about the results of our failed reunion. In all her wisdom, she encouraged us to go back one more time but not ask Geneva for anything, not even for her to accept us. Just give her a nice greeting card, our phone numbers, tell her we love her and let her know she could call us whenever she was ready.

I liked that idea and felt grateful for her advice.

And that's exactly what we did. Jerome made a list of all of our phone numbers for us to leave with our mother. He and I used the hotel printers to make some copies of the pictures we had brought along so that we could leave them with her. Grayson purchased a beautiful greeting card to give her and included some pictures of himself and his family in the envelope.

Little by little, our hope was rekindled and we were emotionally ready to go back and give it another try.

I felt happy that I was not alone in this venture.

We knew that our mother was away from the boarding home at the mental health treatment center, also called "the Center," where they provided games, group counseling, and mental health services, every weekday from early in the morning until late in the afternoon.

Grace LaJoy Henderson

We pulled up to the boarding home about one hour before she was expected to return, with the hopes that we would finally have the chance to speak to April.

My brothers had noticed during our first visit, that our mother almost gave in to me a couple of times and that she seemed intimidated by them. They announced that I should go in alone this time, get her to open up, and invite them to come in once she was comfortable with my presence.

REUNITING WITH MOTHER: A STORY OF TENACITY
Grace LaJoy Henderson

Chapter 3

WILL MOTHER ACCEPT US?

There was still some uncertainty in our minds about whether this woman was really our mother. After all, what if she honestly did not know who we were. I walked into the home all by myself, strolled into a room where two women were sitting and asked if one of them was April. They said, "April went out for lunch about three hours ago and has not returned."

I told them I was there to see Geneva. Before I could tell them who I was, they both exclaimed, "You look just like Geneva!" I told them I was her daughter, and that my brothers and I had found her after forty-nine years. Furthermore, that we had traveled all the way from Kansas City to reunite with her. I explained we came here last night and she refused to talk to us, or to accept us as her children.

The women looked at me with compassion in their eyes. They told me Geneva had not come back from the center, but she would be back in about one hour. They introduced themselves.

Miss Adams was the housekeeper. She told me I was beautiful and that I had hair just like Geneva's, which made me feel proud. She said Geneva was nice, quiet, did not bother anyone and takes care of herself. "She talks to me every evening," Miss Adams said proudly.

The other woman, Miss Davis assured me Geneva would talk to me. "She is just older. She doesn't know. Don't worry, she'll talk to you." She told me Geneva comes to her whenever she wants cigarettes and that she loves to smoke.

Miss Adams took me to see Geneva's bedroom. She had a smile and a proud look on her face as she told me how she made up the bed and how she cleans my mother's room every day.

When I was in her bedroom the night before, trying to reunite with her, the mood was intense. So, I had only noticed the three beds. However, during this showing, more details stood out.

The walls had a light color paint and there was a large piece of framed artwork hanging on the wall next to her bed. There was a four-drawer dresser, two nightstands, and one closet, which Geneva shared with her roommates. The bed cover looked clean, the floor was shining and the room was free of clutter. After admiring the bedroom, we walked back to the room where we had come from.

Miss Davis suggested something that would definitely make my mother to talk to me. "If you bring her cigarettes, she will sit with you and talk."

Miss Adams added that it would also be nice for me to bring her some coffee, shampoo, and soap.

Miss Davis agreed that those things are okay but insisted that cigarettes were what she really wanted. As I was leaving, Miss Davis gave me an empty cigarette carton. "When you go into the store, just show them this," she said. "Ask for *cherry*, that's her favorite kind."

They both assured me I could purchase all of the items at the corner store just down the street. Just like everyone else we had encountered who worked for the boarding home, Miss Davis and Miss Adams were very patient, kind, caring, and showed concern for us having a successful reunion with our mother.

I said goodbye to them as I walked out of the front door and back to the car, where my brothers were eagerly awaiting my return. I told them what Miss Davis and Miss Adams had said about the cigarettes. Initially, they were skeptical until I explained further. Then, we all agreed to take a trip to the corner store and buy whatever was necessary to get her to talk to us.

We purchased an entire carton of her favorite brand of cigarettes, coffee, shampoo, lotion, deodorant and a bar of soap. Then we drove to a local restaurant to get a bite to eat. We went back to the boarding home and, again, I stepped out of our vehicle and proceeded to walk up to the front door.

Miss Davis was outside, walking away from the house towards me. She told me Geneva was not there yet. She pointed to a street corner and told me to look out for a big blue bus to pull up there very soon; and that Geneva would be walking off of it and going into the house.

We sat in the vehicle, intensely watching the corner and waiting for the bus. While waiting, Jerome gave me a list of all of our phone numbers he had made back at the hotel. He told me to be sure to give it to our mother. Grayson handed me the envelope, which included the greeting card and his family pictures. At this point, we were not sure how things would go when I went in there.

Would she accept me when I went in alone?

Would my brothers get an opportunity to go in?

Or would we go back home rejected and dejected?

Finally, the big blue bus pulled up and stopped at the corner, just as Miss Davis had said. The door flew open and out walked all the residents of the boarding home, one person at a time. Eventually, Geneva stepped down the stairs of the bus and limped across the street towards the boarding home. Just then, I remembered how April had told me there was something wrong with my mother's hip.

"That's her!" we exclaimed. I climbed out of the car and walked towards the house. She was wearing the same black jeans, black skullcap and grey fleece jacket under the black leather coat she had on the evening before; and she was carrying a plastic grocery bag in her hand. Her limping prevented her from walking very fast so I caught up with her as she was walking up the stairs of the house.

I said, "Geneva, hi." She looked at me and attempted to walk faster to get away from me. However, her hip pain would not allow her to walk any faster but she continued walking into the front door of the house. I wasn't to be dejected so I continued to walk behind her. "I brought you some things, some cigarettes and stuff. Can we sit down and talk?" I implored.

She stopped walking, turned around, looked at me, then looked at the bags I was carrying. Then she said, "No. I don't know you. I'm not going to talk about my life."

I said, "I just want to talk. I won't ask you about your life, okay? I'll just give you some stuff and you don't have to tell me anything that you don't want to share."

There happened to be a male resident, standing directly inside of the doorway, who heard my conversation with my mother. He looked down at the bag with a look on his face that said, "I don't know what her problem is, but if she does not want those cigarettes, I will take them." She kept walking and didn't say anything else, and I continued to follow her as she walked to the door of her bedroom.

I said, "We will just talk. I will have to respect the fact that you don't want to talk about your life, okay?"

She said, "No, I don't talk to anybody about my life."

I said, "I'll respect that. I understand."

Her bedroom door was locked because all room doors stay locked at all times. She turned to go ask one of the workers to let her in. As she walked into her bedroom, I walked in behind her.

She went over to sit on her bed in the exact same spot where she had rejected us the night before. At the same time, I was standing up pouring all the items my brothers and I had bought on to the bed next to hers. I noticed her eyes light up when she saw all of the cigarettes, but she still did not warm up to me at all at that point. She continued to keep her guard up as she looked at me with a very serious, untrusting look on her face. I continued to pour out the items.

I told her Miss Davis and Miss Adams had told me some of her favorite things.

The mention of Miss Davis and Miss Adams seemed to cause her to relax slightly.

"They both said I look just like you," I told her.

She looked at my face as if to see if she could see a resemblance between her and myself.

"They said my hair was just like yours," I continued.

She glanced up at my hair as if to see if she thought I had hair like hers. It was at that moment that I began to feel like she was warming up to me just a bit.

"I am really happy to have finally found you," I told her. "It has been my dream to find you and take care of you."

I sat down on the bed where I had poured the stuff.

"Here is a list of our phone numbers that Jerome made for you. After we go back to Kansas City, you may call us if you need anything or if you just want to talk."

I showed her my birth certificate and pointed to her name to show her she was my mother. I showed her my copy of her own birth certificate and pointed to her name and her parents' names. She took it and studied it very carefully.

I asked her if she had her own copy.

She shook her head, "No."

I told her she could have that one, and asked for her permission to take a picture of it for me to keep since that was the only copy I had, and it was an original, certified copy.

She nodded her head, "Yes," and handed it back to me.

I whipped out my cell phone and snapped a picture of her birth certificate before handing it back to her.

"I brought some pictures of your children and family. Would you like to see them?" I asked.

She nodded her head, "Yes."

First, I gave her the greeting card and family pictures from Grayson. She opened the envelope, read the card then slowly, patiently and quietly looked at each picture.

Finally, she said something!

"Is this Grayson?" she said as she gazed at a picture.

I said, "No, that is Grayson's son."

Looking at a picture of Grayson's wife, she asked, "Is this you?"

"No that is Grayson's wife."

She continued to look at each and every one of Grayson's pictures very carefully, with much interest. It was at that point, I felt like she was beginning to warm up a bit more. I also knew she was not ready to allow my brothers to come in to meet her. So, I texted them to let them know she was looking at pictures.

When she finally finished looking at the pictures of Grayson and his family, I pulled out some more pictures. I showed her a picture I had of my father with my siblings and me when I was four years old. She held it in her hand and stared at it for a few moments.

She asked me if our father was still alive.

I told her he had passed away back in 1991.

She said, "Are you sure?"

I said, "Yes."

I went on to tell her some of the things that happened with our family after she left. I told her that my father ended up leaving us in a house alone to go work in Florida, and we ended up in foster care.

REUNITING WITH MOTHER: A STORY OF TENACITY
Grace LaJoy Henderson

She said, "Oh yeah?"

The look on her face told me she was not happy to hear that, and I detected that she was experiencing some mixed feelings. The first was a feeling of surprise that my father actually left us. The second was a feeling of hurt for us ending up in foster care. The third was a feeling of disappointment with him for not being the dependable parent that he purported to be while she was still with us.

A moment later her countenance changed as if she was thinking she should not be judging him or saying anything bad about him to me. Yes, I detected all of that just in her facial expressions! I was surprised to see the looks of concern on her face since she had left us and never came back.

It was hard for me to believe she actually cared about what happened to us after she left.

After that, I handed her some pictures of my children and myself. As she looked at them, I told her their names, ages, and what they did for a living. Then she handed the pictures back to me. I took them, but I handed a select few of them back to her to keep. She set them on top of the stack she had made while looking at the pictures of Grayson's family.

Then to my surprise she asked, "What about Terrance?"

Nobody had mentioned my brother, Terrance's name to her.

I felt amazed because this was the first sign of her showing that she actually knew who we were! This made me feel a little more confident that this woman was indeed my mother.

I pulled out some pictures that I had of Terrance and handed them to her. She looked at them with great interest. Noticing that I had not shown her any pictures of his family, she asked, "Does Terrance have any kids?"

I said, "No, he is married though, but I do not have any pictures of his wife."

I finished showing her all of the pictures I had of Terrance.

She looked up at me and said, "What about Danisha?"

Again, I felt amazed because no one had mentioned Danisha's name to her either! Nevertheless, I pulled out some pictures that I had of Danisha and her children. I showed her some pictures of Danisha as a little girl, as a teenager and as an adult. She seemed to take a special interest in one of the pictures; the one in which Danisha was nineteen years old and suited in her Army Uniform. She stared at it a lot longer than the rest, so I told her she could keep that one.

When she was finished looking at all of the pictures I had of Danisha, I showed her some pictures of Carla and her children. Then, I mentioned to her that we did not know where Carla was. She seemed genuinely concerned about Carla missing.

She said, "That's weird that nobody knows where she is!"

REUNITING WITH MOTHER: A STORY OF TENACITY
Grace LaJoy Henderson

When she said that, it gave me a bizarre feeling in my heart because she, herself, left her family and nobody knew where *she* was for almost fifty years! So, I did not understand why she thought it was weird that we did not know where Carla was. Once we were done talking about Carla and looking at pictures of her, my mother surprised me once again.

I was stunned when she asked, "What about Grace?" when I had been sitting there talking with her and showing her pictures for over an hour!

I said, "That's me. I'm Grace!"

She looked at my face as if to see what I looked like. It was at that point when I realized that maybe she honestly did not know who we were the evening before; and maybe she was not purposely denying us; and maybe she truly needed to be sure of who we were before talking to us.

When I really thought about it, I never did introduce myself or tell her who I was. I just walked up to her, said hello and followed her into the house and into her bedroom while telling her I had brought her some things and asking her if we could talk. I just assumed she knew exactly who I was. However, I learned a valuable lesson about reuniting with a long lost loved one after an entire five decades: you have to start from square one and be patient with the person.

Since I had already showed her pictures of my children and myself earlier, I took this moment to ask her if she thinks she will ever come visit us in Kansas City.

She blushed, turned her head to the side, laughed and said, "You're rushing me."

I laughed with her, then I apologized for rushing her. However, seeing her laugh made me realize how very important the pictures were in jogging my mother's memory and helping her to understand who we were. I was even wishing I had brought more.

Chapter 4

REUNITED

I felt like now that the pictures had helped her to recollect her memory, this would be a good time for my brothers to come in. I asked her if I could call my brothers in to talk with her.

She looked afraid and said, "No, not yet, I have some business I have to take care of before I can meet them."

I told her that they traveled a long way just to see her and they would feel sad if they had to go all the way back home and not be able to talk with her. I told her that if they do not get to meet with her while we were in town, there might not be another opportunity.

She said she was not ready.

Feeling afraid that she may never be ready. I asked her if I could ask them to come in one at a time; and assured her they would not ask her anything about her life.

She said, "No, not yet! I need to see them first."

I knew she was feeling nervous and confused so I told her that was why I wanted to bring them in, so that she could see them.

"So, may I call one of them in now?" I asked.

She looked at me with a nervous look on her face and did not say anything for about thirty seconds. Then, her face looked less afraid and she said, "Ok."

I became excited and asked her which one of her sons she wanted to reunite with first.

She said, "Wait, not yet! I'm not ready. I have to take care of my business."

At that point, I very gently reminded her that she said it would be okay if they came in one at a time.

She said, "Oh yeah, okay."

I asked her once again, which son she wanted to reunite with first.

She said, "Umm, Grayson."

I told her I would go get him out of the car and I would be right back. Excited, I hurried out to car where my brothers were anxiously waiting, and told them she was ready to meet Grayson.

My announcement was met with confusion as they all seemed perplexed as to why she only wanted to meet Grayson. They asked me if she knew who we were now and if I was sure she was actually our mother.

In that moment, I had to focus on several things:

Getting Grayson in to the house to meet Geneva, before she changed her mind.

Explaining that she was more comfortable meeting them one at a time, and she chose Grayson as the first.

Calming their valid concern as to why I believe she is actually our mother.

Calming Jerome's disappointment about her choosing to meet Grayson first instead of him.

I quickly told Jerome I believe she asked for Grayson first because he sent in the card and pictures.

Grayson humbly asked, "For real? She specifically asked for me?" As he was opening the car door and stepping out onto the sidewalk.

I said, "Yes," and quickly explained to Jerome and Terrance that our mother was not comfortable with all of them coming in at once. I also rapidly told them that she specifically asked about Terrance and Danisha without me ever telling her their names. Then I rushed off to walk with Grayson.

We walked into the house together, went back to Geneva's bedroom and knocked on the door. She opened the door, we walked in, and she sat back down on her bed.

Smiling, Grayson walked over to our mother.

He gave her a hug and a kiss and she happily accepted. Grayson was careful not to ask her anything about her life. He talked to her about some fond memories he had held about her over the years. Specifically, he reminisced about a time when he was a little boy and he gave her some money because he knew she needed it. He told her that he and his family were doing well and that he was able to provide her with a better life if she so desired. He told her how much he loved and missed her.

The whole time, she looked at him and nodded her head in a "yes" motion, giving a smile every now and then.

Grayson ended his time with our mother by asking her if he could take a picture of her.

She said, "Yes."

Feeling jealous, I asked mother if I could have a picture with her.

She said, "Okay."

So, I sat beside her, she straightened up her cap and Grayson took the picture. Then Grayson took the picture that he wanted of her by herself. Mother seemed more comfortable and happily allowed us to take the pictures.

During the exciting picture-taking moment, after sitting next to her for the picture, it dawned on me how very small my mother's stature was. For a few moments, I wondered how my seven-foot tall father was able to bring himself to hit this tiny woman. She could not have been any taller than five feet two inches.

After Grayson enjoyed mother for a few more minutes, I asked mother which of her sons she wanted to see next.

She said, "Oh okay. I want to see Devon."

So, I asked Grayson if he would go out to the car and ask Jerome to come in. Jerome's middle name is Devon and my mother remembered him as Devon, but we now call him Jerome.

Grayson said his goodbyes to mother, then went outside to the car and sent Jerome in.

After a few minutes, Jerome knocked and I let him into the bedroom. He walked over to where our mother was sitting and gave her a big bear hug and a great big kiss and was very happy to see her.

She had a humungous smile on her face.

Like Grayson, Jerome was also respectful in not asking her any personal questions. Instead, he told her how much he had missed her. He reminisced about how he used to call her "mommy" when he was a little boy.

With a happy look on her face, she said, "All of my kids called me mommy."

Sitting on the bed next to hers, he recollected how she instilled in him a sense of spirituality and that he strives to be a good person today because of it. He recalled how she was a great cook and that she made the best homemade rolls and cookies.

She said she was not sure she agreed she was a good cook, but she certainly had a huge grin on her face the whole time he was talking about it.

Jerome told her he was a good cook, too.

She said, "Oh yeah?" and asked him what he could cook.

He told her he baked pies really well and that he cooks full holiday meals, complete with items like turkey, dressing, macaroni and cheese, greens, and corn bread. He even told her about the few times when he invited me over to his home to partake in the delicious home-cooked meals.

"You can ask Grace. She has been over for holiday dinners," he bragged.

At first, I teased him by saying, "He can't cook." Then, I immediately confessed I was just joking and that he was actually a great chef.

Jerome went on to tell our mother that he was doing well for himself. He showed her pictures of himself, his son, his house, his truck and his wife. He expressed how much he loved and cared for his wife. Then, he actually called his wife using the video chat feature on his phone to let our mother see her and talk with her.

"You are beautiful!" Jerome's wife said.

The compliment caused our mother to smile and even blush a little. It gave me a warm fuzzy feeling, too!

While they were chatting, one of Geneva's roommates knocked on the bedroom door because she wanted to come in. I got off the bed I was sitting on, went to the door and opened it. She walked into the bedroom, went to the closet as if she was looking for something. While standing in front of the closet, she cleared her throat as a way of getting my attention. I looked over at her.

She whispered, "Do you have any change you could give me?"

Realizing I was actually sitting on her bed, I smiled and told her that since she was kind enough to allow me to sit on her bed then I would give her some change. I reached in my pocket, pulled out all of the change that I had and gave it to her.

She said, "Thank you," then left.

After the video chat, Jerome continued to reminisce. He recalled that our mother was a great piano player, that she enjoyed sewing and knitting, and how she loved to polish her fingernails! With a smile on his face he told her, "You used to *always* be sitting at the dining room table polishing your fingernails."

She smiled.

Absently I looked down at her hands, noticing chipped red nail polish on each finger. I guessed she still enjoyed polishing her fingernails.

Jerome's time with our mother ended in yet another photo session.

Just before leaving, he reminded our mother that she had his phone number and she was welcome to call him anytime. He told her that he was capable of providing for some of her needs,

53

and she could feel free to ask. He talked with Mother for a few more moments, then, she was ready to meet Terrance.

Jerome lifted himself off the bed, said his goodbyes to mother, and went to the car to send in Terrance.

Within a few minutes, Terrance showed up at the door of mother's bedroom. I opened the door and in he walked. He began his reunion by giving her a big hug and kiss and telling her how much he had missed her. During his reunion, Terrance asked her if she liked living in the boarding home.

She hesitated, then, said it was okay but she did not like the residents stealing from her. She said she could not have anything of value there and that she used to have a television but it was stolen.

"Well, if you ever want to leave here and come live in Kansas City with us, just call me and I will make it happen," he told her.

"I will let you know," she said.

"I have a lot of business to take care of before I can consider moving."

Whereas, Grayson and Jerome did most of the talking during their reunions with our mother, she had become more comfortable and talked a lot during Terrance's reunion. At the beginning of her reunion with me, she did not want to talk about her personal life. However, by this time, she was sharing some very personal information about herself.

She volunteered the fact that she had ten children.

Terrance and I looked at each other with surprised expressions on our faces.

Then I asked her, "So you had *four* more children after you left?

She said, "Yes."

I told her I was aware of three of them who she left in the hospital, but not the fourth one. I told her about the call my grandmother had received from a hospital, asking if she would take her set of twins after she left them in the hospital. I told her that my grandmother was also informed about her little girl that she left in the same hospital three years before the twins. I asked her if she wanted me to try to find them.

She said, "Yes."

I asked her for the names of the hospitals they were born in and she gave them to me. I asked her for their names and dates of birth.

She told me their first names. She had difficulty recalling their dates of birth, but did her best to give me the correct dates. She said she used to have a list of all of her children's names and birthdates, but she had lost all of her belongings.

REUNITING WITH MOTHER: A STORY OF TENACITY
Grace LaJoy Henderson

This was an amazing moment for me, because I had longed to find the siblings my mother had after she left. However, I had no idea of the children's names and I did not know anyone who could give me even a clue. Therefore, finding them had been close to impossible. Finally, here I was sitting in front of my own mother; and she was telling me the names she gave to each of them. I was able to acquire this long-awaited information directly from the person who named them! Something I never thought would happen in this lifetime!

I felt happy she was being so open after being so cautious at the beginning, but I did not want to hinder that moment. So, I treaded lightly as not to bombard her with all the other questions I had carried in my mind for so many years.

I put a little time, space, and careful consideration between each question. I did muster up the courage, however, to ask her if she ended up marrying the man named Calvin and if she and the additional four children shared his last name.

She said, "Yes," to both questions.

Then I asked her how long she and Calvin were together.

She said, "Two years."

It was very nice to learn details about what her life has been like since she left us five decades ago.

Terrance asked her how she was doing overall.

She said her hip hurts all the time, but otherwise she was doing okay.

I asked her if I could take a picture of her with Terrance.

She said, "Yes," but that she would have to smile with her mouth closed because she was very embarrassed about her teeth.

"I used to have some pretty teeth," she said.

"All of a sudden they just started falling out. I don't know what happened."

She expressed how much she would like to have her teeth fixed.

I told her I knew she used to have pretty teeth because I saw them on the picture of her that I had kept all of those years. I snapped the picture of her and Terrance then she continued to talk openly with us.

As she went on talking, she recited Devon's date of birth. Terrance looked at me in amazement that she actually knew that information. She also recited Carla's middle name. I asked her if she remembered mine.

She said, "I didn't give you one."

I felt very surprised to learn that she did not give me my middle name. I told her it was LaJoy but it did not ring a bell with her. Just then, I remembered how my birth records showed "LaJoy" on the final days of my hospital stay, indicating someone added it at the last minute. So, if my mother did not give me that name, then who did I wondered.

While she and Terrance continued to talk, I veered away in my thoughts, thinking that my grandmother must have given me my middle name. I was silently remembering how she used to correct me whenever I stated it incorrectly. I used to think the correct way to say it was "Joy". However, my grandmother would correct me and say, "Your middle name is LaJoy with a 'La' at the beginning." So, then I began to call myself Grace "LaJoyce."

Again, she would correct me and say, "Your middle name is LaJoy, with no 'ce' at the end." Reminiscing about her insisting I stated it correctly led me to presume that Grandmother was indeed the person who had given me that middle name.

Towards the end of her time with Terrance, our mother had mentioned several times that she needed to go eat her dinner. She was careful not to make us feel unwanted, but she just really wanted to go eat. Finally, we realized how badly she wanted to go eat, so we rapidly began to wrap up our visit. We asked her if she needed anything.

She said, "Do you want to know what I really need? Money!" then she laughed.

We had already planned to give her money, so we both took some bills out of our pockets and gave them to her. We were concerned about giving her cash due to the living environment she was in, because she lived with people who she said steal from her and who had begged us for money. Out of my concern, I asked her if she knew how to protect her money.

She said, "Yes." She kept it in her purse, which she wore strapped around her neck and across her chest at all times.

As we were walking towards the front door to leave, we saw the very large dinner rack. We also noticed there was only one plate of food on it so we guessed it was hers. In hindsight, we realized that if she had not come for dinner when she did, one of the other residents would have taken her plate and eaten her dinner.

After she had secured her dinner plate, I asked her what her favorite food was.

She said, "Fried chicken."

I asked her if she wanted us to bring her some the next day and have dinner with her.

She said, "Yes," with a smile on her face.

Terrance was in agreement with coming back the next day, too. As we were leaving out of the door, she reminded us with excitement in her voice, "Tomorrow at four o'clock, don't forget!"

We said, "Okay."

As we were leaving, we each hugged our mother and gave her a kiss on the jaw. In turn, she gave each of us a kiss on the jaw, too. We proceeded to walk out of the door and joined Jerome and

Grayson in the car. We were talking about the very emotional reunion we had just had with our mother.

Terrance told Jerome, "Man, she knew your birthday!" And nobody had even told her!

He seemed amazed by that, which let me know that just like our mother truly needed to understand who we were, he truly needed to feel sure that she was our mother.

When we told Jerome and Grayson we had promised our mother that we would come back the next day with fried chicken, Grayson was okay with it. My thought was that since we were there to see her, then I expected we would spend as much time as we could with her. Jerome's thoughts were different.

"I will not be joining you all for dinner with Mother tomorrow," he announced.

I believe Jerome only needed the memory of reuniting with her and knowing that she was okay. I believe he found closure after she had accepted us. He wanted memories that he could share with his offspring, nieces and nephews, and he got that.

As he drove us all back to the hotel, I had time to do some silent thinking of my own. I initially felt like since Geneva was my mother, who carried me in her stomach for nine months, she should have accepted me immediately, no questions asked. What I did not think about was this: just like we bombarded her with questions at the beginning, because we wanted to be sure of who she was, she also needed the opportunity to be sure exactly who we were, especially since she had ten children, whom she had been separated from for decades.

She needed to be able to understand whether we were the first set of six children she left in Kansas City, or the second set of four children that she left after her departure from us.

I guess when a person has been living in denial about having children for so many years they do not just snap out of it in one moment.

I had to sit with her, talk softly to her, show her pictures, be kind and gentle and introduce my brothers slowly and carefully, one at a time, while eagerly hoping she would accept each of them before we traveled back to Kansas City.

I felt like we had just had a very productive day!

When we returned to the hotel, we ate dinner then retired to our rooms for a good night's sleep.

REUNITING WITH MOTHER: A STORY OF TENACITY
Grace LaJoy Henderson

Chapter 5

OUR FINAL VISIT WITH MOTHER

That next morning, we ate breakfast together at the hotel restaurant. Then we went back to our respective rooms to rest up before going back to the boarding home for dinner with our mother that evening. While in our hotel rooms, Terrance and I got into an argument over the phone and I was feeling unloved. Therefore, when it was time to go have dinner with our mother, I was so upset that I announced I was not going. After a few minutes of drama, they ended up getting in Grayson's rental car and going without me.

The argument was not related to our mother but, at the time, it seemed huge. Looking back, it was mere sibling rivalry, which had soured my mood. However, at the time it appeared enormous enough to cause me to refuse to visit my mother, whom I had longed to know for forty-nine years.

After they pulled off, I began to think about how it was my idea to have dinner with her in the first place. I thought about how much I really wanted to have this moment with our mother. Most of all, I remembered how badly I wanted to ask her why she left and listen intently as she talked to me about it. So, I hopped into the rental vehicle that Terrance and I had purchased and drove myself to the boarding home.

They went to buy the chicken dinner first, so I arrived at the home before them. I texted to let them know I was there and waited for them to show up so we could all walk in together. I was still feeling sad, but I put on a happy face so that we could all enjoy this final visit with our mother. Finally, they arrived and we walked in at four o'clock, with a large chicken meal, as promised.

One of the workers met us at the door and asked, "May I help you?"

We told her we were there to have dinner with our mother, Geneva, so she gave us permission to proceed. We walked back to our mother's bedroom and knocked on the door. It took her a couple of minutes to open the door. When she finally did, she explained that she had fallen asleep because her hip had been hurting.

She was wearing a red long sleeve top with black pants, and the same black skullcap on her head from the evening before. She wore her black purse strapped around her neck and across her chest. She carried two worn plastic grocery bags, one in each hand. I am not sure what was in the bags, but as I glanced around inside of the home, I noticed pretty much all of the residents carried around their belonging in some type of old worn bag.

Grace LaJoy Henderson

She pranced away from her bedroom with a great big smile on her face and led us into a huge dining room area. It had about ten very long tables with several chairs at each one. This was where the boarding home residents usually gathered to eat their meals, but we were the only people in there at that time. We placed the bags of food on one of the tables.

She mentioned that her hip was hurting and she had run out of pain pills. Grayson and Terrance offered to go to the store and buy her some and she accepted. She told them the brand she liked and asked for the large bottle of extra strength.

They left out of the house and headed to the store, while my mother and I remained seated in the dining area.

"Where is Devon?" she asked.

"He stayed back at the hotel to rest up for his early morning flight home," I responded.

There was a moment of silence, which I broke by asking a heartfelt question.

"Did you ever think about us over the years?"

She said, "Yes, all the time."

She mentioned again that she had ten children and told me she initially only wanted two children, a boy and a girl. She said, "If anybody would have told me I was going to have ten children, I would not have believed them!"

I felt surprised that she said that to me, because it brought up some feelings of rejection inside of me. However, I felt good knowing she was opening up to me. I was able to handle her truth.

At that moment, I remembered how my father would rant about how she did not want all of the children she was having. Yet, she did not believe in birth control or abortion. Hearing her say she never wanted so many children caused me to think about the adverse effect it must have had on her mental illness.

We avoided that subject when she asked me what I did for a living. I told her I had a regular full-time job and that I was an author of several books. I told her I began my writing journey by writing poems as a little girl. She smiled as she told me she used to write poetry when she was a little girl, too. She asked me what inspired me to become a writer. I told her that writing poetry helped me to deal with my feelings growing up.

I told her that everything I experienced as a child inspired me, like not knowing where she was and living in foster care after my father left.

"Is he still alive?" she asked.

I immediately remembered she had asked me that same question the day before; but I answered it as if it were the first time she asked.

"He passed away back in 1991," I told her.

"Are you sure?" she asked.

I told her that I was.

She said she could not believe he had passed away. She began telling me about the people upstairs on "the third floor" who have been saying that her "husband" was still alive.

I asked her "Which husband, Calvin or Father?"

She said my father.

Since she told me she and Calvin were married after leaving Kansas City, it was bizarre to me that she was still referring to *my* father, whom she left almost fifty years ago, as her husband. Furthermore, I knew that there was no "third floor" in the boarding home, so I presumed she was referring to the voices she hears in her head due to her mental illness.

With my brothers still being gone, I thought this might be a great time to ask her why she left.

"Do you remember anything about how things were just before you left Kansas City?" I asked.

She looked at me as if she was afraid to answer that question. She may have a mental illness, but she is very smart. I believe she was very aware that was a loaded question. I think we both knew that if she answered that question, it would lead to me wanting to know more about her time in Kansas City just before she left; In particular, why she left.

Therefore, instead of answering my question, she went back to talking about the people "upstairs."

Finally, my brothers returned from the store with her pain medicine. She took one of the pills right away, then we all sat around talking and eating.

A few minutes later, my niece called my phone number so that we could do a video call between our mother and my sister, Danisha. She entered the video and they were both smiling as they said hello to each other. All of a sudden, my sister asked, "Grace, how do you know this is our mother? She does not look like our mother." I felt speechless because I knew it would take more time than we had to explain how I knew she was our mother. To my surprise, our mother did not seem offended by my sister's doubt. She just asked her a couple of questions, which Danisha answered happily and they said their goodbyes.

My sister actually learned we had found our mother just moments before the video call. Therefore, she had not had the much-needed opportunity to process the information before being face-to-face with this estranged woman. The shocking news of finding our mother had been sprung on her without any prior preparation.

This left me feeling guilty that we had not told her sooner.

You see, we really wanted to take Danisha with us but circumstances did not allow it. We made the difficult decision to travel without our sister, with the intention of using technology to bring her together with the lady who delivered her into this world.

My father had once said, that out of all six of his children, he believed Danisha had the deepest affection for our mother. We did not know how the reunion would go and we did not want to subject her to any rejection if our mother did not receive us.

When our mother finally received us, we did not want to leave without giving Danisha an opportunity to see her and talk to her, since we did not know if or when we would ever be in-person with our mother again. Actually, my niece and I had discussed preparing my sister in advance of the video conversation. We had planned for her to arrive at my sister's place thirty minutes to one hour before the call. However, she arrived later than expected and did not get a chance to prep her mother for this very emotional interaction.

After our mother's chat with my sister, we kept on sitting in the dining area eating our meal and talking.

The worker who had met us at the door knew Geneva was our mother because we had announced it when we first arrived. She did not show a reaction at that time. But, she walked into the dining room with an extremely surprised look on her face.

She looked at Geneva and said, "You never told me anything about having children! I had no idea!"

Geneva looked at her but did not say anything.

The worker left the room and we continued to eat.

This was the second person who had expressed disbelief about Geneva having offspring. I was surprised to learn that denial was how my mother had chosen to cope with leaving all of her children. It seemed not having her children in her life had been difficult for her. It was hard for me to imagine how she must have felt about it. I wondered if maybe she had felt guilt, shame, or embarrassment. But, I did not dare ask her.

We continued to sit at the dining room table talking with our mother, with our chicken meal setting on the table. We had only bought enough food for our mother and ourselves, but we were not eating it very fast because we were spending a lot of time talking and learning more about our mother.

One of the boarding home residents came into the dining area, looked at our food and asked for some chicken. We gave her a piece. She left out of the room and came right back, looked at our food again and said, "I love mashed potatoes and gravy!" So, we gave her all the mashed potatoes and gravy we had left.

When a male resident saw her with the food, he came in and asked for some. Thankfully, we were able to honor his request.

I was very hungry but I had not eaten yet because I was busy conversing. I observed that there were two more pieces of chicken in the box, which I planned on eating when I got a break from talking. When I was finally ready to partake of some chicken, I looked in the box and it was empty.

Grace LaJoy Henderson

Feeling puzzled, I looked around the table and none of my brothers had taken the chicken out of the box. Then I looked over to my right, at the table beside ours, and observed a male resident with a plate of chicken. He was eating it very fast and appeared to be enjoying it very much. I felt a little mystified because the box of chicken was sitting right in front of me, but I did not see the man take it.

I looked over to my left, at the table where my mother was sitting. My brother, Terrance, was standing in front of her. I had a baffled look on my face.

Terrance whispered, "I said he could take it."

The mystery was finally solved. I still felt hungry but I was happy the man was enjoying the chicken.

At that point, with the food being gone, I felt our visit would be over soon. So, I asked Grayson if he wanted to take a picture with our mother.

He said, "Yes."

I took one with my cell phone and one with his. Then I asked Grayson to use my cell phone to snap a picture of me with our mother. I had taken pictures of Jerome and Terrance with our mother the evening before, but not Grayson. As we were taking the pictures, again our mother mentioned feeling embarrassed about smiling due to the condition of her teeth.

Terrance told her that if she moved to Kansas City, it would be easy for us to take her to have her teeth fixed. We could monitor the process and take her to all of her appointments.

She reminded him of the "business" she has to take care of before she could consider moving.

After our photo session, we looked out of the window and noticed it was beginning to get dark. The descending darkness was a cue for us that we should go. As our visit was nearing its end, we all expressed to our mother how much we truly enjoyed our visit with her. We informed her how much we would love to bring her to live closer to us. We voiced our desire to remove her from the boarding home, move her to Kansas City and provide all of her needs. We reminded her that she had our phone numbers and that she could call us anytime.

One of the last things my brother, Terrance, said as we were walking out of the door was, "When you are ready to come to Kansas City just call and say, 'I wanna come.'"

She smiled and said, "Okay."

Each of us gave her a hug just before walking out of the door. When I gave her my goodbye hug, she kissed me on the jaw. Then we left out of the door.

The quarrel Terrance and I had gotten into before coming now seemed insignificant. He, Grayson, and I walked out together, jumped in our separate vehicles, drove back to the hotel, ate dinner, then retreated to our rooms to rest up for our flight back to Kansas City early the next morning.

As we traveled home, we shared our experience of meeting with mother. We all agreed on how nice it would be to bring her to live closer to us. We conversed about how we could place her in a safe environment, where people would not steal from her, where she would not have to carry all of her belongings around in a bag, where we could facilitate the treatment she needs for her hip pain, and where we could take her to have her teeth fixed.

We brainstormed about ways to keep the communication lines open with her and maybe inspire her to move closer when she felt more comfortable, after getting to know us better.

We all agreed it would be best for us to return home, call her every once in a while, send her cards and gifts for her birthday and other special occasions, with the hopes that we could bring her closer to us at a later date. We all realized that our hands were somewhat tied since that final decision would have to be hers. If she were happy to reside at the boarding home, then we should be happy, too.

Even though I agreed with my brothers, I still carried an unsettling feeling in my core. I left feeling disappointed because our mother did not readily accept our offers to move her to Kansas City, to allow us to provide a better life for her.

REUNITING WITH MOTHER: A STORY OF TENACITY
Grace LaJoy Henderson

I was shocked that she preferred to stay in the poverty-stricken place she was living, when we could provide a nicer place. I know she said she had "business" to attend to before she could consider moving. However, I could not help but to wonder if she really had business or if that was just her way of stalling.

However, I had to realize that she had been living there for over fifteen years and while, to me, it looked like a bad place for her, to her it was home. Therefore, I had to accept her desires and just be grateful that I had this awesome chance to reunite with my mother.

The feeling of gratefulness in my heart matched the tenaciousness of my mind. If, by chance, she really did have "business," I felt determined to find out what it was and help her with it. I went back home thinking of ways to get her to move to Kansas City. I would not let what took place on this visit stop my efforts to bring Mother closer to her family.

Discussion Questions

1. Mother talked to the author and Jerome on the phone before they traveled to reunite with her. What reason(s) did she express for not accepting them as her children upon their arrival?

2. What did the author do to try to get Mother to accept them during the very first attempt?

3. What, if anything, could they have done differently to cause Mother to accept them during their first attempt? Discuss your response.

4. The author and her brothers felt rejected and discouraged after the first meeting, but they returned the next day to try again. If you were in their situation, would you have tried to reunite for a second time? Or would you have just gone back home? Discuss your response.

5. Name one or more things the author did to get Mother to finally receive them when they went back the second time.

6. During the second attempt to win over Mother, the author did not give up until Mother agreed to reunite with the brothers. What are your thoughts about this?

7. The author and her brothers offered their mother a "better life" with them in Kansas City. What was Mother's response?

   What are your thoughts about Mother response?

8. Why do you think the author called this book a "Story of Tenacity?"

Questions Teachers Can Ask
Critical Thinking/In-depth Comprehension/Writing Skills/Technology Skills

1. What is the main idea or learning experience of the book?

2. Write your thoughts or feelings about the story or your favorite character.

3. Summarize your favorite part of the book and tell why this was your favorite part.

4. Write about an experience in your personal life and tell how it is similar to this story.

5. Write a summary of the story, highlighting what you think the main issues are.

6. To whom would you recommend this book? Why?

7. How can the information in the story be useful in your life or future?

8. Research a famous or infamous person on the computer who was abandoned by their mother, and write a report about that person's life.

9. Research a famous or infamous person on the computer who suffered from a mental illness, and write a report about that person's life.

Further Discussion Points

Reuniting with Mother indicated some of Geneva's Symptoms, Coping Behaviors, and Treatments for her mental illness. It also indicated some Effects this has had on the author. Below are some excerpts, from the book, that you may use for additional discussion.

Symptoms

Hallucinations. One symptom of Geneva's diagnosis is hallucinations. She often referred to the things she was hearing from "people upstairs on the third floor." Geneva seemed to be having *auditory* hallucinations. Read and discuss the excerpts below.

She began telling me about the people upstairs on "the third floor" who have been saying that her "husband" was still alive. **Page 67**

Furthermore, I knew that there was no "third floor" in the boarding home, so I presumed she was referring to the voices she hears in her head due to having a mental illness. **Page 67**

Abandonment. Geneva only wanted two children, but had a total of ten, and left them all. Read and discuss the excerpts below.

She mentioned again that she had ten children and told me she initially only wanted two children, a boy and a girl. She said, "If anybody would have told me I was going to have ten children, I would not have believed them!" **Page 65**

At that moment, I remembered how my father would rant about how she did not want all of the children she was having. Yet, she did not believe in birth control or abortion. Hearing her say she never wanted so many children caused me to think about the adverse effect it must have had on her mental illness. **Page 66**

Coping Behaviors

Denial. When the author and her siblings went to reunite with Geneva, she denied them at first, then, later accepted them. Read and discuss the excerpts below.

She looked at each of us again, and just when it appeared she might actually accept us as her children, she said, "You are not my people. Anybody can come in here and say they are my people." **Page 25**

"You all are strangers. I don't talk to strangers about anything personal. I'm not giving out any information unless I know who I am talking to." **Page 25**

We assured her she did not owe us anything, that we were not looking for any apologies, that we loved her and just wanted to see her. She said, "No, I don't trust that," **Page 25**

Denial. It appears Geneva may have been in denial about having children for all of the years she had been gone. Read and discuss the excerpt below.

But, she walked into the dining room with an extremely surprised look on her face. She looked at Geneva and said, "You never told me anything about having children! I had no idea!" Geneva looked at her but did not say anything. The worker left the room and we continued to eat. **Page 65**

Avoidance. Geneva said, on several occasions, that she had "business" to take care of before she could reunite, move closer, or move forward with her relationship with the author and her siblings. Read and discuss the excerpts below.

Then, her face looked less afraid and she said, "Ok." I became excited and asked her which one of her sons she wanted to reunite with first. She said, "Wait, not yet! I'm not ready. I have to take care of my business." **Page 48**

He told her that if she ever wants to leave there and come live in Kansas City with us, just call him and he would make it happen. She said she would let him know, but that she has a lot of business to take care of before she could consider moving. **Page 50**

Terrance told her that if she moved to Kansas City, it would be easy for us to take her to have her teeth fixed. We could monitor the process and take her to all of her appointments. She reminded him of the "business" she has to take care of before she could consider moving. **Page 72**

The feeling of gratefulness in my heart matched the tenaciousness of my mind. If, by chance, she really did have "business," I felt determined to find out what it was and help her with it. **Page 74**

Avoidance. Geneva often referred to the "people upstairs on the third floor" to avoid talking about events that were stressful for her. Read and discuss the excerpt below.

Therefore, instead of answering my question, she went back to talking about the people "upstairs." **Page 67**

Treatments. Treatment for Geneva has included:

- **Medication**
- **Psychosocial Intervention**
- **Hospitalization**

Medication. The mental illness that Geneva has affects her actions, thoughts and feelings. It causes her to see the world differently from someone who does not have a mental illness. This means she may try to avoid taking her medication. Sometimes it may be challenging to get her to cooperate. Read and discuss the excerpt below.

Ashley claimed that Geneva never talks to her and that she usually has a hard time getting her to take her medication, whereas April had given us a completely different account. **Page 27**

Psychosocial Interventions. Geneva receives this type of treatment through the boarding home where she lives and the mental health treatment center where she attends daily. Between the two programs, she is able to manage her mental illness and live somewhat of an independent lifestyle. Read and discuss the excerpt below.

Miss Adams took me to see Geneva's bedroom. She had a smile and a proud look on her face as she told me how she made up the bed and how she cleans my mother's room every day. **Page 36**

Effects on the author

Feeling Hurt. The author felt hurt after Geneva denied them.

Witnessing her living in a state of poverty and suffering from a mental illness helped me to understand why she left us. Nevertheless, it still hurt deeply. I had always blamed my father for her leaving, but after this failed reunion, I was placing all the blame on her. **Page 30-31**

These *Further Discussion Points* are only a few things that stood out for the author from her own story. Did you see any additional Symptoms, Coping Behaviors, Treatments or Effects on the author as you read the book? If so, please free to discuss them.

FINDING MOTHER SERIES

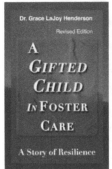

A Gifted Child in Foster Care:
A Story Resilience – REVISED EDITION
In this book, Dr. Grace LaJoy shares her life story of being deserted by her mother, living in foster care, and ending up in a gifted and talented class while still in foster care. She recalls her life story before, during and after foster care. The *Finding Mother Series* was written as a sequel to this book.

Finding Mother After Five Decades:
A Story of Hope
Grace LaJoy's determination pays off when she finally finds her mother who abandoned her at age two. Discover the specific details about her intriguing journey in **Finding Mother after Five Decades,** BOOK 1 of the *Finding Mother Series.*

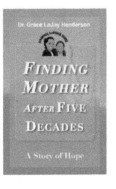

Reuniting with Mother:
A Story of Tenacity
What happens when Grace LaJoy and her siblings come face-to-face with their estranged mother after 49 years? How does she receive them? Find out in **Reuniting with Mother,** BOOK 2 of the *Finding Mother Series.*

81

After the Reunion:
A Story of Acceptance
After a very emotional reunion, Grace LaJoy has two concerns to address with her long-lost mother. What are her concerns? Does she get the answers she needs from her mother? Find out in **After the Reunion,** BOOK 3 of the *Finding Mother Series.*

Diary of Emotion:
Thoughts and Feelings
After reuniting with her mother after 49 years, Grace LaJoy toils with an array of thoughts and feeling. She reveals them all in **Diary of Emotions,** BOOK 4 of the *Finding Mother Series.*

Available in softcover and Kindle eBook
Collect them all at Amazon.com
Ask for the series in
bookstores and libraries
www.gracelajoy.com

PRAISES FOR THE FINDING MOTHER SERIES

Grace LaJoy Henderson's *Finding Mother Series* is a revelation. It is a gift to discover an author who can write so honestly—and with such vulnerability—about the joy and pain of reuniting with a parent after a 49-year separation. Henderson never glosses over the frightening or disappointing parts of her story. But her compassionate, unwavering voice, as she uncovers the long arc of her mother's life, is itself a triumph. **~Whitney Terrell, Associate Professor of English, University of Missouri-Kansas City**

"The author's emotional honesty and the balancing of positive and negative emotions is what makes this series work." **~Phoebe Shanahan, MA in English Literature**

"The Finding Mother Series will inspire readers to *feel* their feelings. It stirs people in similar situations to be at peace, but at the same time seek growth, in the midst of their circumstances." **Arica Miller, LMSW, School Social Worker**

"The *Finding Mother Series* displays a perfect example of how one triggering event can cause conflicting emotions. Throughout the series, the author experienced hope *and* despair, excitement *and* apprehension. Two, totally opposite emotions both at the same time. However, both were completely justified! This range and transition of emotions is what drives the entire *series*. Secondary students will absolutely benefit from reading this collection of books." **~Jacob Kelow, M.S.Ed., Secondary School Counselor, Kansas City Public Schools**

PRAISES continued →

"The *Finding Mother Series* is written in a very powerful, real and authentic voice style. The author's honesty shines through her writing. Although the author's sadness throughout the story is quite palpable, her attitude towards her mentally ill mother is full of grace and understanding despite the fact that she had abandoned her. This is a clear and honest work." **~Fay Collins, Writer-Editor**

"The *Finding Mother Series* is a beautiful sequence of books. The author's reunion with her mother is very well documented." **~Phyllis Harris, Former Missouri State Director, Parent Information Resource Center**

"The author shares her personal story in an authentic way. Easy reading. Flows well." **~Ila Barrett, Behavioral Therapist, Jacksonville, FL**

"The Finding Mother Series is an inspiration to all who have faced abandonment by a parent. Grace LaJoy's truth validates her determination never to extinguish the fire, which burned in her soul to find her mother." **~ Dr. Gwendolyn Squires, Former School Principal, Kansas City Public Schools**

"Reading this series may help others who long to be reunited with their parents." **~Dr. Mary E. McConnell, Educator, University of Missouri-Kansas City**

"The Finding Mother Series will touch many people who are in this same situation, but who may not have the forgiveness in their hearts that the author and her siblings have. It is going to touch lives in more ways than you can imagine." **~Jean Smith, Dallas, TX**

"I strongly believe that this series will heal a lot of broken hearts and act as a source of encourage, advice, guidance and counsel for people in such scenarios; both children and adults." **~Ken J.**

ABOUT THE AUTHOR

Dr. Grace LaJoy Henderson
is the author of over thirty books.
Her foster care story, *A Gifted
Child in Foster Care: A Story of
Resilience, Classroom Set* and her
children's book series, *The Gracie
Series*, are currently being used in
public and charter schools.

Pearson Higher Education published two chapters from her
foster care story in a college textbook.

She has earned a Doctorate in Christian Counseling, a Master's of
Education in Guidance and Counseling, and a Master of Arts in
Curriculum and Instruction. She has also earned a Bachelor's
degree in Social Psychology.

Dr. Henderson managed a contract with the Missouri Children's
Division, in which she provided court ordered mentoring for
foster youth, supervised parent-child visits and parent education.
She has served as psychology and college success instructor as
well as academic coach. Outside of higher education, she is a
keynote speaker, workshop leader and guest author at schools,
libraries and other organizations. Newspapers, radio and
television has featured her publications and her story.

REUNITING WITH MOTHER: A STORY OF TENACITY
Grace LaJoy Henderson

CPSIA information can be obtained
at www.ICGtesting.com
Printed in the USA
LVHW011524210520
656177LV00006B/821